# Coaching The Soccer Brain
# Using Small-Sided Games

21 Ways to Manipulate Small-Sided Games In Order to Increase Game Intelligence, Raise The Soccer IQ, Develop Thinkers & Improve Overall Decision Making Abilities

By Marcus DiBernardo

## Introduction

I started out coaching over twenty-five years ago and its safe to say a whole lot has changed since then. Even when I was a player, it was the physical side of the game that was emphasized, along with being brave and committed, words like cognition were meant for psychology class and not the soccer field. Maybe once in a while the coach would shout, "what are you thinking", undoubtedly not to teach us anything but more as a reprimand then anything else. The idea of developing the soccer the brain wasn't something I was ever exposed to as player and young coach. However, there were pioneers back then; Wiel Coerver was spreading the message of the importance of technical training, but the link between technical training, physical training and the brain was never fully developed or discussed. This motivated me to make it my mission re-think player development on every level, from youth to adult. I ended up creating a coaching methodology that is specifically designed to develop the soccer brain. The theory and applications behind my work are presented in detail in my five book series "Cognitive Soccer Instructors Diploma Course Manuals" #1-5, these are also sold on amazon.com. This book focuses primarily on ways you can train the soccer brain by playing small-sided games using different variations, rules and conditions. In order to be successful in SSG's (small-sided games) the players will need to problem solve and figure out solutions to each exercise, the exercises will ultimately become the teacher. The coach can certainly step in to ask questions (to guide the players), make corrections or adjust a rule or condition. However, it is important the coach does not try and over-coach the players, allows enough time for players to become comfortable with the exercise before making changes and keeps a good overall flow to the practice. SSG's are so effective because players get to experience a variety of different meaningful situations which they have to strategize and problem solve collectively as a unit and as individuals to solve. This in turn will ultimately develop the soccer brain! Don't get me wrong, expert feedback from a talented coach during training is necessary, but it is even more critical that the coach understands how to set-up exercises that will allow players to learn on their own as well. If the exercise is breaking down, the coach should have the tools to make an adjustment, so the correct level of challenge is present. If the players are not challenged enough, the coach should be able to make an adjustment that will increase the games difficulty. I can go into detail about the importance of novelty in training, sweet spot of learning, the value of unique soccer experiences, the benefit of healthy stress in training, the use of priming, the power of questions and much more, but the purpose of this book is to give coaches the tools to make any SSG into a "Brain Development Game". If you are interested in learning more about Cognitive Soccer Development or wish to become a "Cognitive Soccer Certified Instructor" please visit my website at www.soccersmarttraining.com

Feel free to email any question of comments to coachdibernardo@gmail.com

**Table of Contents**

## Small-Sided Games Using Variations, Rules & Conditions

Before we jump right into the actual SSG's with different variations, conditions and rules; I wanted to cover some of the basic ways you can adjust SSG's. Most of the exercises in this book use a "neutral" or "plus" player. All that means is whichever team is in possession of the ball the "plus" player is on the team in possession. You can allow the "plus" player to score or not allow it. Feel free to use more than one "plus" player if needed. The idea of adding a "plus" player is to make the game flow easier with the team in possession having more passing options. If the game is 1-touch only, the use of "plus" players helps the flow of the game noticeably. As with all the tools I will be mentioning, the "plus" player is just another tool that gives the players a different experience and can change the make-up and strategy of the game. Varying the numbers on each team is another way to adjust the game. Playing 7v6 is different than 7v7 and much different than 7v7+2(plus players). Each of these examples will require different strategies by the players to be successful in SSG's. The size of the field is a tool that can increase or decrease the difficulty of SSG's. The shape of the field is another factor that will influence strategy. Touch restrictions are an obvious tool that can increase or decrease difficulty. Placing unique restrictions like, no straight forward passes, 1-touch back passes only or no square balls are all great was to challenge the players, while placing them unique situations that they will learn from. Allowing 2-touch on turnovers while playing 1-touch games has a major impact on flow of the game and strategy. Playing 2-touch on the turnover followed by the next 2 passes being mandatory 1-touch and then free play is yet another variation that can help players develop their soccer brain. The next

21 SSG's presented in this book can be manipulated a thousand different ways. The idea is to show you the possibilities so you can go out build on those ideas. However, it is very important that you have an understanding of the effect each rule, condition and variation has on the game. A top coach will be able to go into a SSG and change it, so the players are in an optimal learning zone, constantly being challenged and motivated while developing their soccer brain! Feel free to change any of the SSG's in this book in terms of numbers, "plus" players, field size, goals, keepers and any of the conditions. The SSG's in the book are here to stimulate your ideas and provide you with coaching tools that will have you developing your player's brains in no time!

# Exercise #1

## 5v5+1 Channel Possession

**Grid:** 35 x 25 yards + (5 yard wide channels)
**Players:** 5v5+1
**Instructions:**
The objective of this SSG is to get the ball into one channel and then into the opposite channel. Once the team plays into both channels consecutively the team receives 1 point. The use of channels in this SSG serves to encourage build-up & possession play. The team in possession must be patient, as they work the ball successfully into both channels without losing possession. The players should be patient and develop a rhythm while in possession. This exercise makes excellent an SSG all the way up to a full 11v11 game.
**Coaching Tool:** Using two 5-10 yard wide channels to build possession play, while developing a playing rhythm.

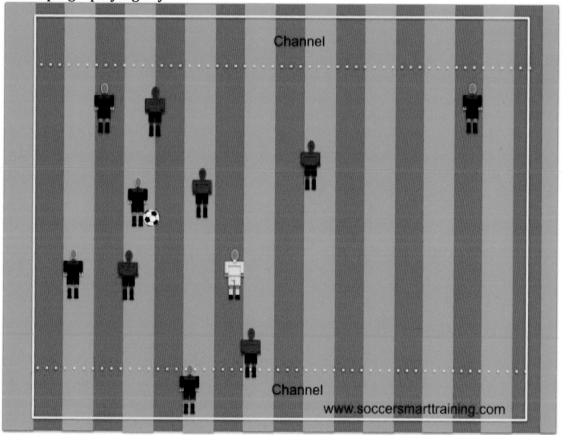

# Exercise #2

## 5v5+1 Channel Possession To Goal (One Direction)

**Grid:** 35 x 25 yards + (5 yard wide channels)
**Players:** 5v5+1
**Instructions:**
This exercise is the exact same as exercise #1 but small goals are now added to one end line. Once a team has played into both zones without losing possession they can score on either small goal. The only way to score a point is by entering both channels and then scoring on one of the small goals. By bringing goals into the game teams will have the chance to score after executing successful build-up play. Using the goals is a logical progression and variation; the players must adapt and figure out what the best strategy is to be successful with this new variation. Having two goals also doubles the amount of decisions the players can make when attacking compared to just using one goal.

**Coaching Tool:** By adding goals to a game it provides a direction and changes the strategy. By adding two small goals it offers players more attacking decisions on the ball. If you were to add one big goal it will change the strategy again. All these variations are positive and help to develop the soccer brain.

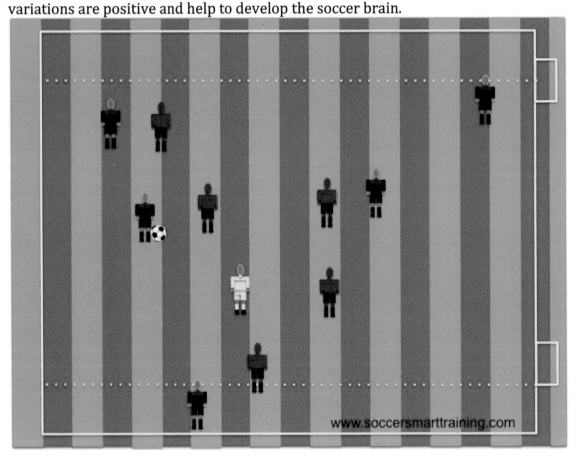

www.soccersmarttraining.com

# Exercise #3

## 5v5+1 Channel Possession To Goal (Two Directions)

**Grid:** 35 x 25 yards + 5 yard wide channels
**Players:** 5v5+1
**Instructions:**
This exercise is similar to exercise #2; the difference now is there are goals on each end line. The red team will attack one direction and the black the other. The rule is still in effect that you must enter both channels before attacking. However, you can adjust the rule to bring about different qualities. Example: Have the teams enter both channels plus one more channel order to score (team will have entered channel total of three times). This will force even more build up and possession play. You can also reduce the condition to entering just one channel and then allowing the team to score. This will result in a quicker game with less build-up. It is important to see what the effect of changing the condition or rule will have on the game.
**Coaching Tool:** Adding goals for each team offers even more specific direction to the exercise. Understanding how to manipulate the game by changing the rules and conditions is critical.

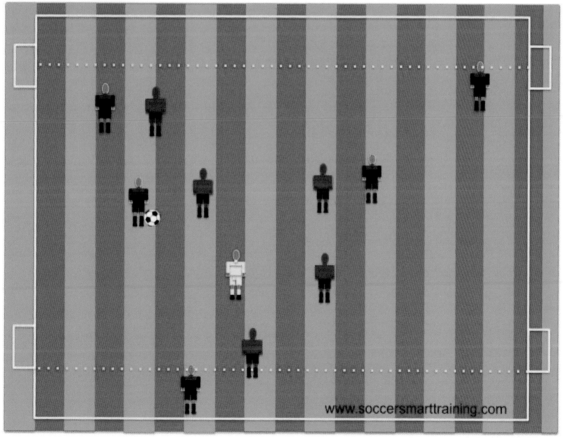

www.soccersmarttraining.com

## Exercise #4

### 5v5+1 Rotation Possession

**Grid:** 35 x 25 yards
**Players:** 5v5+1
**Instructions:**
This SSG works on rotating the ball quickly from one side of the field to the other in order to generate an attack down the channel. The team in possession must play through one of the red gates before attacking goal. By simply adding these two gates it completely changes the players strategy. The team can play beyond the gates but in order to score the ball must be played through the gates first. Once possession is lost the new team in possession must play through a gate before scoring. This is a very good exercise for players that play in central positions like the defensive center midfielder, whose main job is to switch the ball from side to side.
**Coaching Tool:** Using two gates to train quick ball rotation, while attacking down the channels.

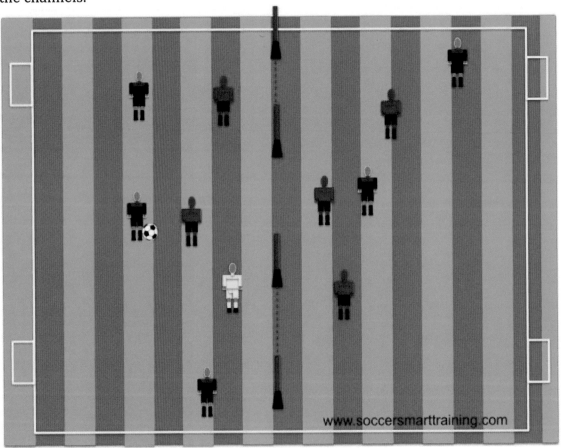

www.soccersmarttraining.com

# Exercise #5

## 5v5+1 Rotation Possession (Long Pass)

**Grid:** 35 x 25 yards
**Players:** 5v5+1
**Instructions:**
This game is same as exercise #4 but with the added condition that all passes through the gates must be from behind the blue markers. Example: if the black team plays a penetrating ball through the red gate, it must be hit from behind the blue marker on their side of the field. This condition forces longer range passing and penetrating balls. Teams can play the ball anywhere on the field but in order to score it must first travel through either red gate from a pass behind the blue marker.
**Coaching Tool:** Using a marker to train longer range penetrating passing.

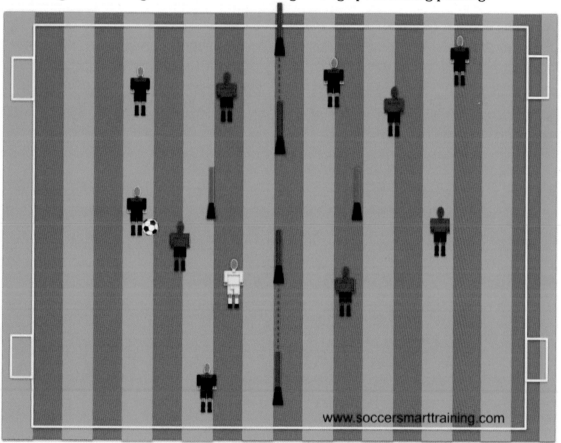

www.soccersmarttraining.com

# Exercise #6

## 5v5+1 Long Penetrating Passing

**Grid:** 35 x 25 yards
**Players:** 5v5+1 with each team having 5 end line players (21 total players)
**Instructions:**
This game uses markers to encourage long-range penetrating passing. The black team in possession can only score a point if they hit a pass on the ground from behind the black marker to one of the their teammates standing on the end line (black players located far side). The red team can only score by hitting a pass from behind the red marker to a red teammate on the far end line. You can vary the rules by having 12 completed passes counted as a point or letting the yellow "plus" player score. What should end up happening in the game is teams will be forced to work the ball all around the field to create space and opportunities to score from behind the marker with a longer pass.
**Coaching Tool:** Use of markers to increase players passing vision and encourage longer-range penetrating passing.

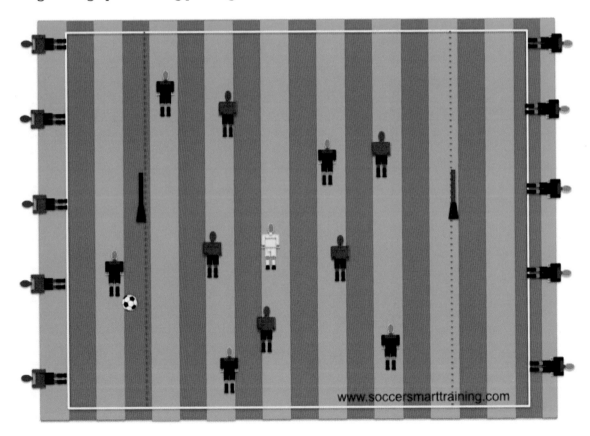

www.soccersmarttraining.com

# Exercise #7

## 5v5+1 - 4 Pass Possession Scoring

**Grid:** 35 x 25
**Players:** 5v5+1 with each team having 5 end line players (21 players total)
**Instructions:**
This exercise is the exact same set-up as previous exercise. However, the objective is now shorter passing and build-up play. The black team must complete a minimum of 5 passes without crossing the red marker before hitting a penetrating pass to score into a teammate on the end line. The red team will do the same but they will need to complete a minimum of 5 passes before crossing over the black marker and then score with a penetrating pass. Feel free to adjust the number of passes required before hitting the penetrating ball. You can also adjust the distance of the markers to make the space larger or smaller. Rotate inside and outside players every couple of minutes.
**Coaching Tool:** Using markers to work on build-up possession play.

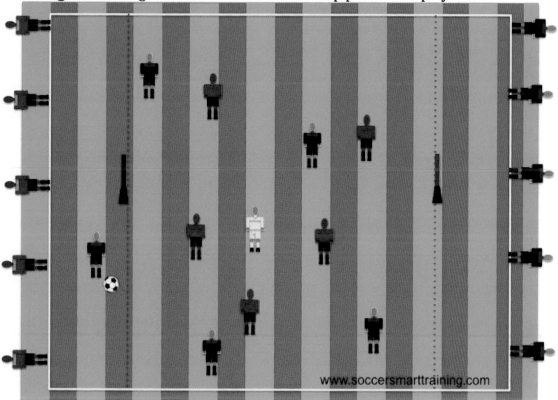

www.soccersmarttraining.com

# Exercise #8

## 5v5+1 Pressure Possession & Compactness

**Grid:** 60 x 40
**Players:** 5v5+1
**Instructions:**
This SSG creates a high-pressure possession environment that demands quick movement of the ball. Place a line down the middle of the field that divides the field in half. The rules of the game are simple, both teams have to be located in one half of the field, one team is pressing while the other is trying to work the ball out of the half to score on either of the two small goals in the opposite half. The team trying to work the ball out is not allowed to cross into the opposite half of the field to score until the ball crosses the half line. If the ball crosses the half line, all the players on both teams must sprint into that half (the half of the field that the ball is in). The team defending can't drop off defenders to stop an attack until the ball crosses the half line as well. There are many variations from touch restrictions, large goals with keepers, 6 small goals, 3 "plus" players for 1-touch only SSG, determine the type of penetrating ball allowed (no air balls) etc.
**Coaching Tool:** Using a line that cuts the field in half to work on quick ball circulation under pressure, high pressure defending, team compactness, transition and timed attacking movements.

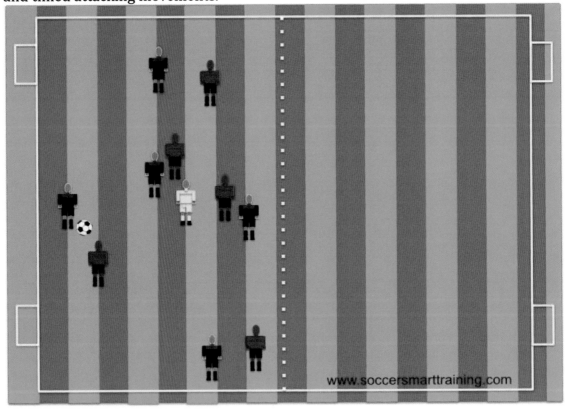

www.soccersmarttraining.com

# Exercise #9

## 6v6+1 (1-Touch Box)

**Grid:** 45x40
**Players:** 6v6+1
**Instructions:**
This SSG uses a box marked in the middle of the field that designates a 1-touch zone. Anywhere outside the box is unlimited touch. Using the box requires players to think at least one pass ahead and encourages passes to be played through the middle to be transferred quickly out wide. Players can combine in the middle but it must be 1-touch. The rhythm of passing in the middle square will be very fast. Players can go anywhere on the field at anytime, both inside and outside of the box.
**Coaching Tool:** Using a 1-touch box in the middle of the field to encourage quick play and transition of the ball out wide.

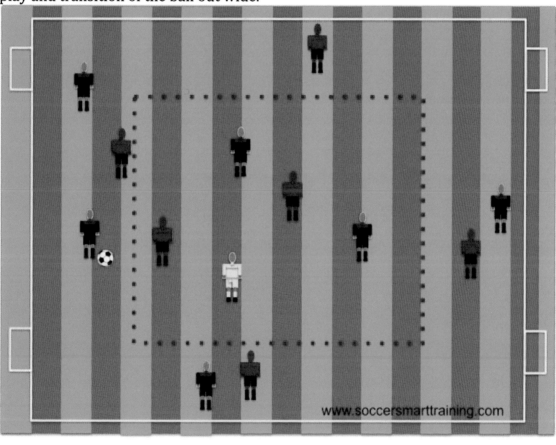

www.soccersmarttraining.com

# Exercise #10

## 5v5+1 Zone Play

**Grid:** 45x35 yards
**Players:** 5v5+1
**Instructions:**
The field is divided into four equal zones in this SSG. The team in possession can't stay in one square (zone) more than 2 passes; the 3rd pass must be played out into a new square. By playing this way it forces quick ball circulation using the entire four squares. Teams do not have to wait until the 3rd pass to play into another square; they can play it out on the 1st or 2nd pass as well. Variation: require 3 passes in the square with the 4th pass to be played out to another square. By changing the number of passes it now requires more support in possession in the small-square and shorter range passing.
**Coaching Tools:** Using two lines to divide the field into four equal squares. This will encourage ball circulation and support off the ball using the entire field.

www.soccersmarttraining.com

# Exercise #11

## 5v5+1 Zone Play To Goal

**Grid:** 45x35 yards
**Players:** 5v5+1
**Instructions:**
This game is very similar to exercise #10 with the addition of small sided goals. Teams play a regular game and with the condition that the 3rd pass must be played into a different square or shot at goal. Feel free to adjust the conditions to create different challenges.

**Coaching Tool:** Using two lines to divide the field into four equal squares. This will encourage ball circulation using the entire field with the end result being a shot on goal.

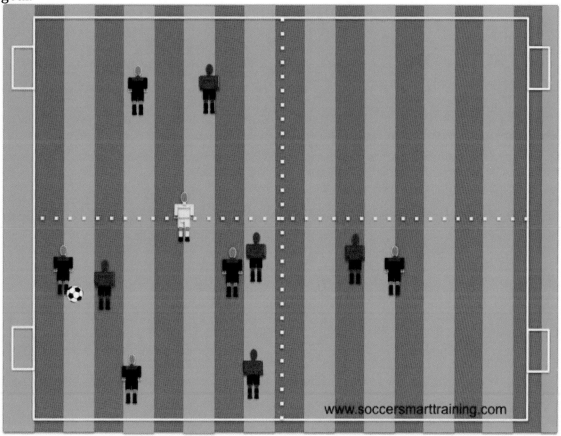

www.soccersmarttraining.com

# Exercise #11

## 6v6+1 Zone Play Variation To Goal

**Grid:** 45x35 yards
**Players:** 6v6+1
**Instructions:**
This exercise is the exact same as exercise #10 with the addition of an extra 2 squares, the rules remain the same.

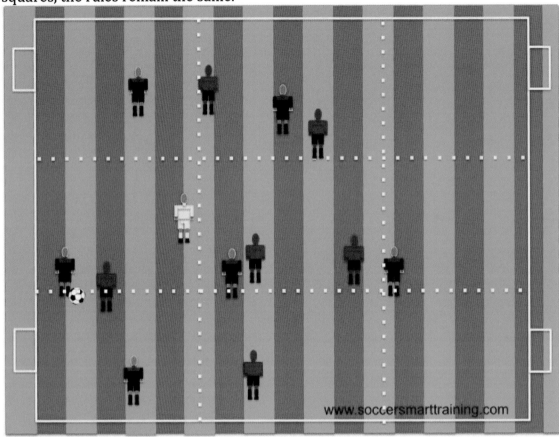

www.soccersmarttraining.com

# Exercise #12

## 6v6+1 No Forward Straight Passing

**Grid:** 45x35 yards
**Players:** 6v6+1
**Instructions:**
This SSG has a field that is divided into vertical channels. The condition of the game is that every pass must leave the channel the passer is in. This will encourage diagonal passing and general ball circulation. Feel free to add touch restrictions and variations. Example: All back passes must be 1-touch.
**Coaching Tool:** Creating a field of vertical channels to encourage diagonal passing and general ball circulation.

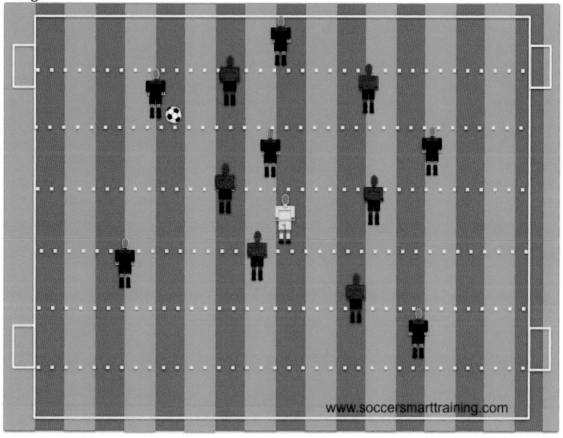

www.soccersmarttraining.com

# Exercise #13

## 5v5+1 Attacking Three Lanes

**Grid:** 45x40 yards
**Players:** 5v5+1
**Instructions:**
The field in this SSG is divided into 3 vertical lanes.  The condition in the game requires the attacking team to have a player in all 3 lanes in order to score a goal.  If a goal is scored and the team in possession did not have a player in each of the 3 lanes, the goal will not count.
**Coaching Tool:** Using two lines that divide the field into 3 vertical channels and requiring the attacking team to fill all 3 lanes.  This coaching tool teaches attacking width.

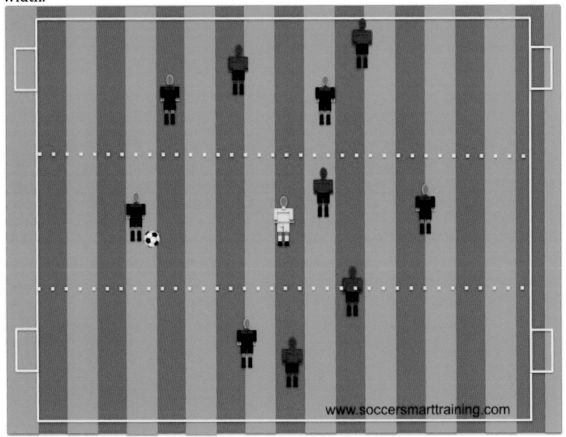

www.soccersmarttraining.com

# Exercise #14

## 5v5+1 Defensive Compactness

**Grid:** 45x40 yards
**Players:** 5v5+1
**Instructions:**
This is the exact same as exercise as #13 but now we focus on the defensive team instead of the attacking team. The defensive team in red must fill the lane with the ball and the next lane over, leaving the far lane empty. When the ball is in the middle lane they can occupy all 3 lanes, but they should still stay condensed towards the middle lane. The exercise teaches defensive shape and compactness. You can add off sides to the game, touch restrictions, using regulation goal+keepers and any other variations you like.
**Coaching Tool:** Using two lines to divide the field into 3 vertical channels that teach defensive compactness.

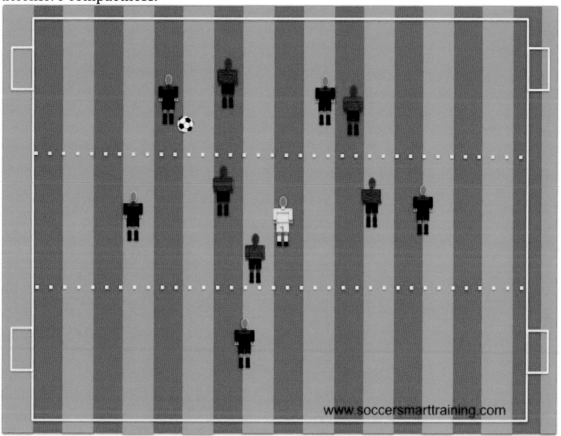

www.soccersmarttraining.com

# Exercise #15

## 5v5+1 Counter

**Grid:** 70x35 yards
**Players:** 5v5+1
**Instructions:**
The field is divided into 3 horizontal sections (20/30/20). Both teams start in the middle section. Once the team in possession completes 4 passes they can hit a penetrating ball into the attacking 1/3 releasing 3 attackers, the defense can release 2 defenders. The attackers have 3 passes to score in the attacking 1/3 with 2-touch restriction. No players can cross over into the attacking 1/3 before the ball crosses into the attacking 1/3. Variations: change number of passes before hitting penetrating ball, use one goal instead of two, send 2 attackers and 1 defender.
**Coaching Tool:** Divide the field into three vertical zones to train counter-attacking movements.

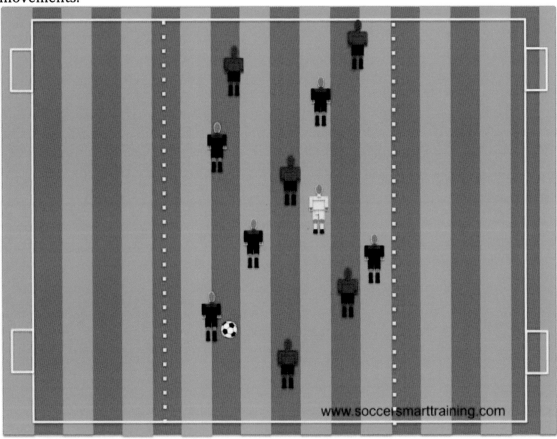

www.soccersmarttraining.com

# Exercise #16

## 6v6 Line of Confrontation

**Grid:** 70x40 yards
**Players:** 6v6
**Instructions:**
The field is divided into 3 zones (20/30/20 – yards).  The red team can send one defender over the red line (line of confrontation) to pressure the black team.  The black team can only send one defender over the black line (line of confrontation) to pressure the red team.  These two lines of confrontation simulate an actual game that uses defensive zonal tactics.  The game is a regular game with whatever condition you wish to impose.  The line of confrontation teaches team to drop off defensively as a unit.

**Coaching Tool:** Use two lines to mark out the line confrontation for each team.  This will give the game a realistic shape and feel in terms playing against zonal defenses that hold a general line.

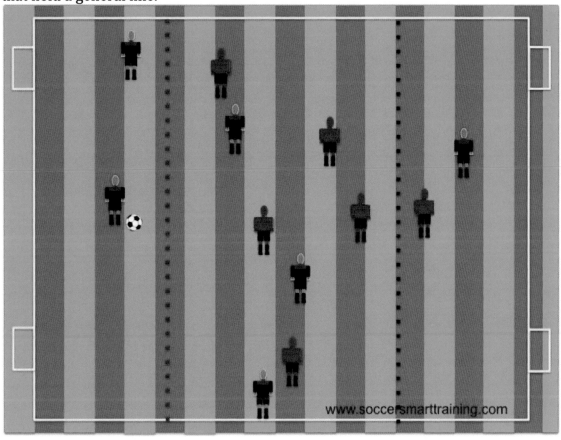

www.soccersmarttraining.com

# Exercise #17

## 7v7+1 Overloads

**Grid:** 60x40 yards
**Players:** 6v6
**Instructions:**
The field is divided into 3 sections (15/30/15 – yards). This is an overload SSG that is directional. The "plus" player goes from zone to zone helping the team in possession. The "plus" player can score and hit penetrating passes to the next zone. The only restriction is that only the "plus" player can travel from zone to zone while the other players must stay in their zones. The idea of the exercise it to create overloads and learn to use overloads to keep the ball, create penetrating passes and score. The game is played directional like a normal game scoring on goal, however players must remain in their zones as the "plus" player creates the overload.
Variations: play to large goals with keepers and use touch restrictions.
**Coaching Tool:** Divide field into 3 zones to create overloads using a "plus player". Dividing the field is an excellent visual for players to actually see how the overloads can be utilized.

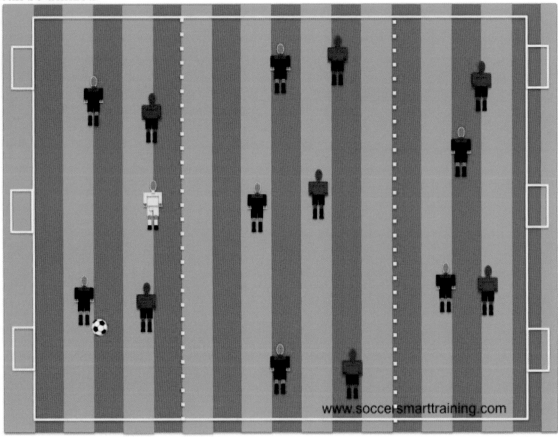

www.soccersmarttraining.com

# Exercise #18

## 6v6+1 Overload Channels

**Grid:** 60x40 with 10 yards channels on each side.
**Players:** 6v6+1 & 2 GK's
**Instructions:**
This SSG is another overload game. The overloads will occur in the wide channels.
The team in possession can have 2 players enter the wide channel and the defending
team is allowed 1 player in the channel. At any time if a player comes out of the
channel a new player can pop in (strategy involved). The team in possession in the
channel is limited to 2-touch. Variation: Make it mandatory to enter both channels
before scoring. Using the channels forces overload training.
**Coaching Tool:** Make two channels to encourage overloads in wide areas.

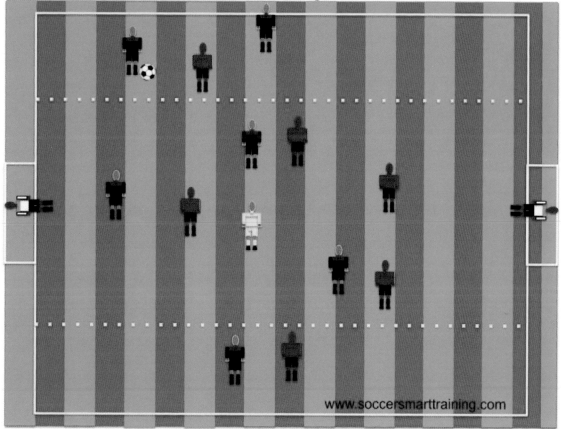

www.soccersmarttraining.com

# Exercise #19

## 5v5 – Attacking Support

Grid: 60x40 yards
Players: 5v5
Instructions:
The field is divided into three 20x40 yard sections. The only rule is that the team in possession must have a minimum of 2 players in the middle zone when the ball is in the attacking 1/3 in order to score a goal. The idea is to have the players organized in a balanced attack shape with support back in order to swing the ball if needed.
**Coaching Tool:** Divide the field into 3 equal sections to work on attacking support play.

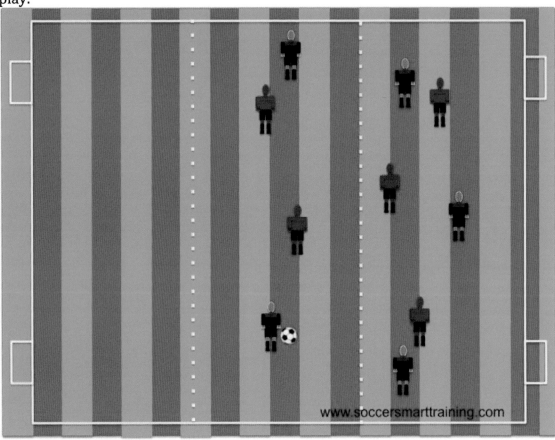

www.soccersmarttraining.com

# Exercise #20

## 5v5+2 1-Touch Zone To Goal

**Grid:** 60x40 yards
**Players:** 8v8+2
**Instructions:**
The field is divided into two equal sections with 7v5 (really 5v5+2 "plus" players) on one side with the ball and 3v3 on the other side waiting. The team in possession plays 5v5 +"plus" players. If the team in possession looses the ball, the other team will try and play it across to their teammates wright away. Two players from each team and the two "plus" players will cross-over quickly into the next grid to try to score – this will make a 5v5+2 in the attacking grid at all times. The game focuses on quick transition and using the overload of 7v5. If a goal cant be scored on quick transition, the team needs to open-up in attacking organization (be patient in possession if the counter isn't on) to make use of the 7v5 overload until an opening to score presents itself.

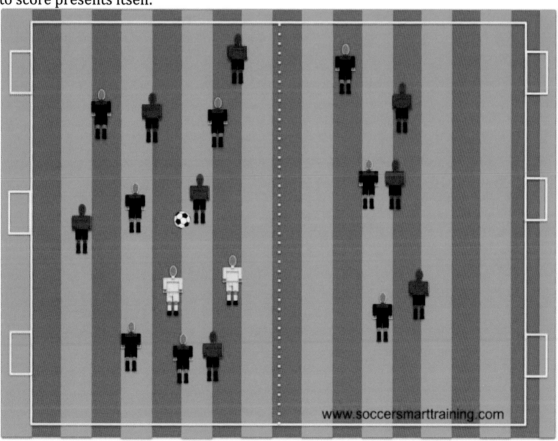

www.soccersmarttraining.com

# Exercise #21

## 6v6+1+GK's – No Horizontal Passes

**Grid:** 60x45 yards
**Players:** 6v6+1+Gk's
**Instructions:**
The field is divided into 9 horizontal sections. This SSG is played like a regular game with keepers, the only condition is players are not allowed to pass the ball in the same horizontal channel; the ball must travel into another horizontal channel. This game will encourage diagonal and vertical passing to be successful.
**Coaching Tool:** Use vertical lines to create horizontal channels, which encourage diagonal and horizontal passing.

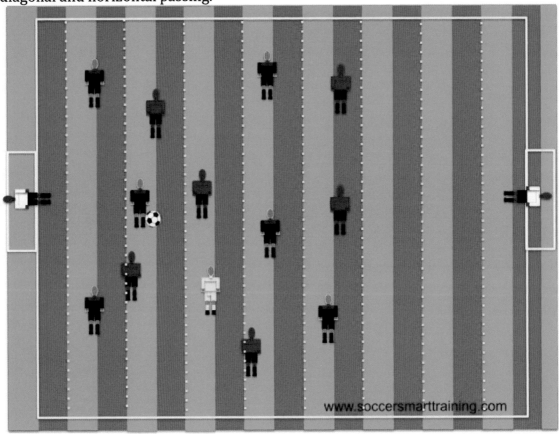

www.soccersmarttraining.com

Printed in Great Britain
by Amazon